The Breath Capital

SNEŽANA ŽABIĆ

THE Breath Capital

New Meridian

Library of Congress Cataloging-in-Publication Data

The Breath Capital
Authored by Snežana Žabić

ISBN-13: 978-0-997603828
2016910708

Contents

Fake City / 37

Introduction

The Breath Capital records points of bodily contact in urban environments where eye contact is tacitly forbidden, but where we breathe each other's molecules in and out.

The Breath Capital borrows construction material from texts I consume and translate, old and new, be they poetry, theory, science, or music and other arts. The barrel in which this material is stored has a double bottom: underneath the English language hides my native tongue, Serbo-Croatian, which broke apart during the Balkan wars of 1990s. Now this language is considered to be four languages: Bosnian in Bosnia and Herzegovina (where my paternal grandparents were form), Croatian in Croatia (where I'm from), Serbian in Serbia (where I lived and even had a bit of a literary career in 1990s), and Montenegrin in Montenegro (where I traveled every summer as a kid). I don't feel welcome or comfortable in any new version of the language, and so American English has become the default: it fits much better, although ambivalence remains.

The Breath Capital is haunted by 20th-century Europe, but it exists in the Unites States in the 21st century, amid the current drama of late-capitalist class struggle tied to the past and present racial and gender politics. To extend the well-known metaphor by William Carlos Williams, my poetry is a machine that condenses the amorphous and oftentimes banal vapor of human achievement and error in order to produce liquid or even icy verse.

S.Ž.

Artist's Statement — ROOMS: *stories from the timespace*

Series of collages and drawings mostly portraying obscure rooms inhabited by undefined presences. An attempt to create an emotional and sensory narration through usage and juxtaposition of abstract shapes, unconnected associations and depiction of sounds and movements.

Dunja Janković

Hle, to jsem já. Souhra představ těchto papoušků s kouzelnými jmény. /
Look, it's me. The interplay of images of these parrots with magical names.

Vítězslav Nezval, "Papoušek na motocyklu"/
"Parrot on a Motorcycle", 1924

On the other hand, when I think of how often the matter of poetry is narrowly
defined as emotion and perception only, the term "conceptual poetry" begins to
look very attractive, at least as a corrective.

Rosmarie Waldrop, "Some Ambivalence About the Term 'Conceptual
Poetry'" in *I'll Drown My Book: Conceptual Writing by Women,*
edited by Caroline Bergvall, Laynie Browne, Teresa Carmody, and
Vanessa Place, 2011

Most of my writing has died before birth, because ideas came to me while
cooking or doing other things for family.

Rati Saxena in *A Megaphone: Some Enactments, Some Numbers,*
and Some Essays about the Continued Usefulness of Crotchless-
pants-and-a-machine-gun Feminism, edited by Juliana Spahr and
Stephanie Young, 2011

Pneumonitism

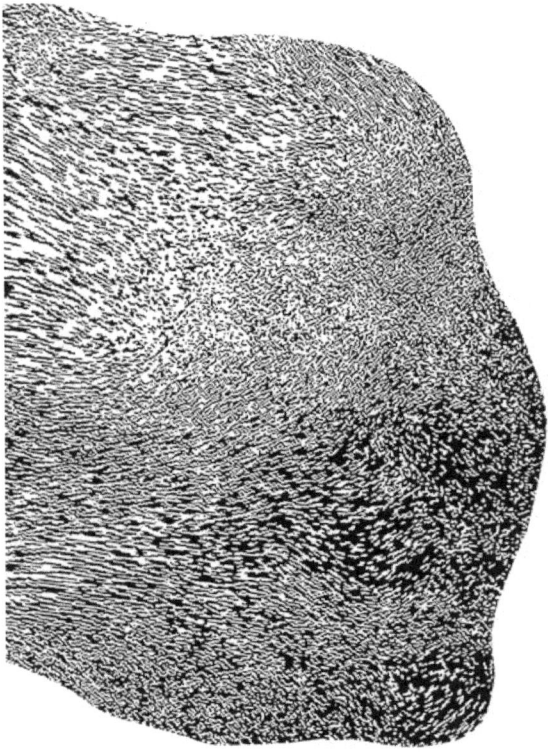

pneumonitis, n.

Brit. /ˌnjuːməˈnʌɪtɪs/, U.S. /ˌn(j)uməˈnaɪdɪs/ ancient Greek πνευμον-, πνεύμων lung (see pneumono- comb. form) + post-classical Latin -itis
Inflammation of the parenchyma of the lung, (in later use) esp. of non-infectious (allergic, physical, chemical, etc.) origin; an instance of this.

Oxford English Dictionary Online

pneumonitism, n.

Brit. /ˌnjuːməˈnʌɪtɪsm/, U.S./ˌn(j)uməˈnaɪdɪsm/ ancient Greek πνευμον-, πνεύμων lung (see pneumono- comb. form) + post-classical Latin -itism

A sick movement in art and literature seeking to express solidarity with revolutionary interventions by any of a number of different techniques, including the irrational juxtaposition of realistic images, the creation of mysterious symbols, and Gertrude Steinism; the texts of pneumonitism are mostly composed on buses and trains of the Chicago Transit Authority.

The Manifesto of Pneumonitism

with Tasha Fouts, via Vítězslav Nezval and Karel Teige

My beautiful little sisters, my hospital quiets, my past century boulevards. Theirs is the old way of writing bound by digestion. It was endless war, late capitalism, money.

A new art is no longer art. Slits of drool and dank, mold of pressed grooves, of grime, of penny holes and screws. This is the trumpeter's mouth piece: metal tonguing skin.

Their gratification, a world of the image. Their muse, ask the parrot. This needs to be said directly. I was looking in vain for a clear-sighted web designer, when fever, having liberated itself from the medical database, took pyrotechnics in its arms and began dancing. My beautiful little sister, my satellite dove.

Through knock and knock and unknock and burn. Reburn.

This needs to be said directly: all of my senses are functioning. Mental health of the 22nd century is the premise of the future poetry.

My mouth's been made implicate, defective apparatus lathed in process and thought. Will the body too suffer the tongue's confusion of noise.

You darling fire eaters. It's the ears that awake you to life. The tune of a glorious fun house. Constant noise of highways. Dull roaring that kills me.

The mouth loves the crack of the whip. Virgin forests and fat verse on the corner. Blue colors of workers' uniforms, those vertical skies. New gardens and grape-picking, my birds.

What need, then, for a turtle? Your sound is so furious. The squirrel's frantic-frantic prayer hands know.

Work: what precedes. Ask the trumpeters and the fire eaters. Ask the parrot on the motorcycle.

Spirit

Movements slow down with   breathing
in   beat beat beat   out   beat beat beat
a mouse   no   a wiping rag   no
a cricket   no   but something   divides this "spirit"
"spi" is asleep and "rit" is a marshland   no peace   no walk
through catalog nostalgia   a vineyard   nobody knows of
               white linens strewn about my room
                         that's right, my room by the damn vineyard

Limbs

Hard to remember now: May cherry explosions of Europe's riots of nineteen thirteen. Or was it twenty-four. My antenna points nowadays to steel fire escapes and this world's women who build makeshift instruments and wrestle survival out of nothing.

Class enemy no. 1 wears a padded grey dress, skillful under a big red umbrella and titanium stormy sky purchased on the global marketplace.

My broken antenna points to this world's firebirds in a handful of kids' bedrooms south, north, west, and east of Lake Shore Drive. Hundreds of miles in each direction, avant-garde of footwork and alignment, flow and angled poses, rage in limbs.

Lungs

Lungs of aspen, birch, pine, spruce, and fir trees are my ancient others. I witness a crowd of atomic pilgrims in New Mexico only on TV. It's hard to remember now. I understand the pull of the desert. Where slim men in tropical worsted suits once tested the bomb. I understand the fear, the pull, the sanatorium of dry air.

Soot

Irving Park and Central taste of a stranger's cigarette smoke. I'll write in my black notebook how he was an older man, an archetype in a grey trench coat, he was an inhale, an exhale, our mixed molecules in my mouth.

You come to work each day, and machinery submits to your control; you sift flour, and notice particles suspended in the cold air.

Snow falls on young weeds, and the sidewalk cracks. It's the last heavy snowfall before spring. Overnight, in the wrecked photosynthesis, the factory breathes oxygen kneaded into soot, leaves a message to be deciphered later, much later.

Recipe

Rise in the morning.

Find springtime, solar energy, naked bodies, and sloping rocks beneath Dubrovnik.

A year and a day later, 366 observations of marine and citrus life.

Three sips of water with a bit of salt and lime juice.

Three lines of poetry.

Perform three movements of your choice, dance of breath flow.

Return to bed, lower your body onto the still warm spot.

October Tanka

Beyond the red egg in the east—
horizon of water.
May the egg roll away
from the event, crash
into a new universe.

Paper Finger Manifesto

two hens would do
a string of lights on a tavern wall
carousel's last spin for the day
two hens and an orange olympia
beaks pecking at the keys
percussion of typebars
ribbon and the paper finger

Poison Buttons

This is the last poem

poetry is work
and muscle memory
fabric and a belt
and the ribs

This is the last dress
I'll conflate with a poem
I keep becoming
more mechanical
less binary code

more association:
like watermelon
or pineapple

This is not my last
piece of fruit

my overload of juicy
interiors under hard skins
stickiness and
heavy smell this side
of fermentation

I cultivate ideas
until they ferment
into poison

and that's what
I'll wear

poison

after the last dress
the last poem

With It

If the interior scroll unfurls and plugs itself into the current
to power bicycle wheels better than my legs and breath,
do we start a gallery in the back of a truck
that runs on vegetable oil?
You may question the cycles of production,
but march can't be your monarch any more
than my patchwork banner can be a parachute
to help me land after each of our riots.
When my movement begins to flag,
a trap door will open in the concrete below us.

A Red Fragment

imagine a red fragment
entering my flesh
　　　—kari edwards

a red fragment commutes
from the west side
a red fragment works
the help desk at the art institute
she used to be a red ribbon around
the lion's neck (the left one)
and then a red rope in front of seurat

her boots are filthy
her shadow is art deco

once she was robbed on the train
almost raped another time
but the assailant's palms
got slashed open
when he grabbed her neck
a red fragment's neck
is is is a saw

The Body Academy Workbook

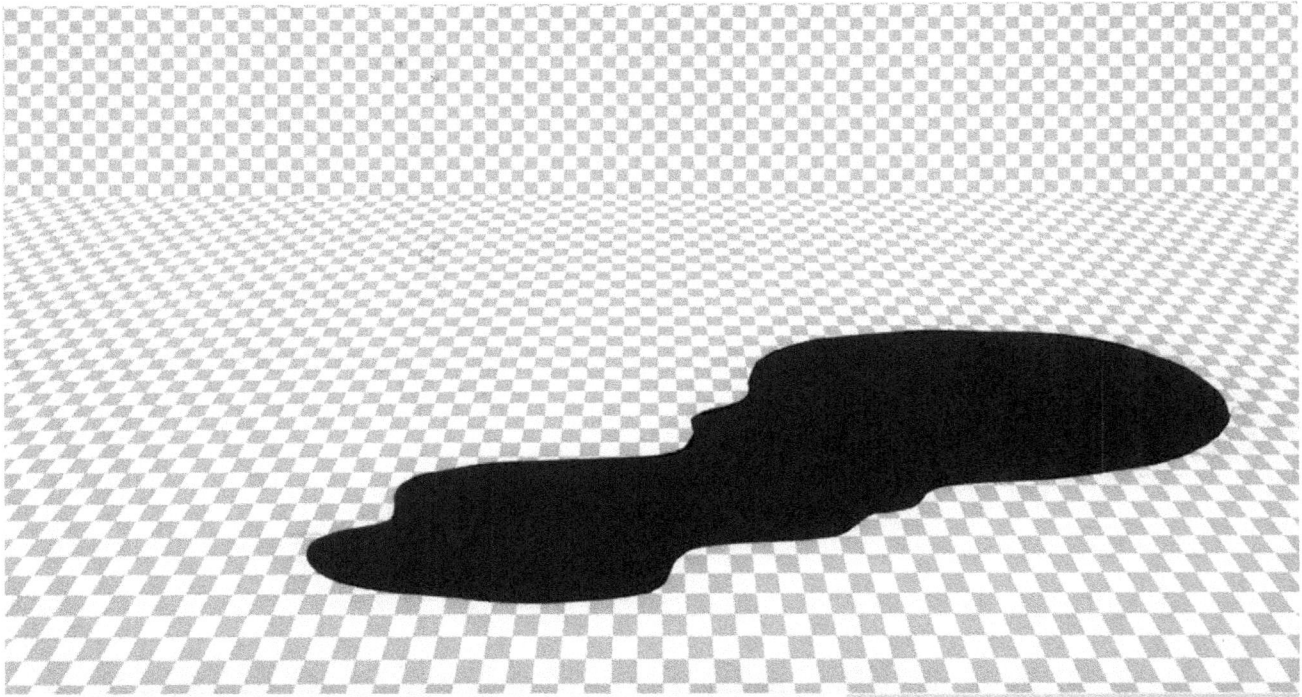

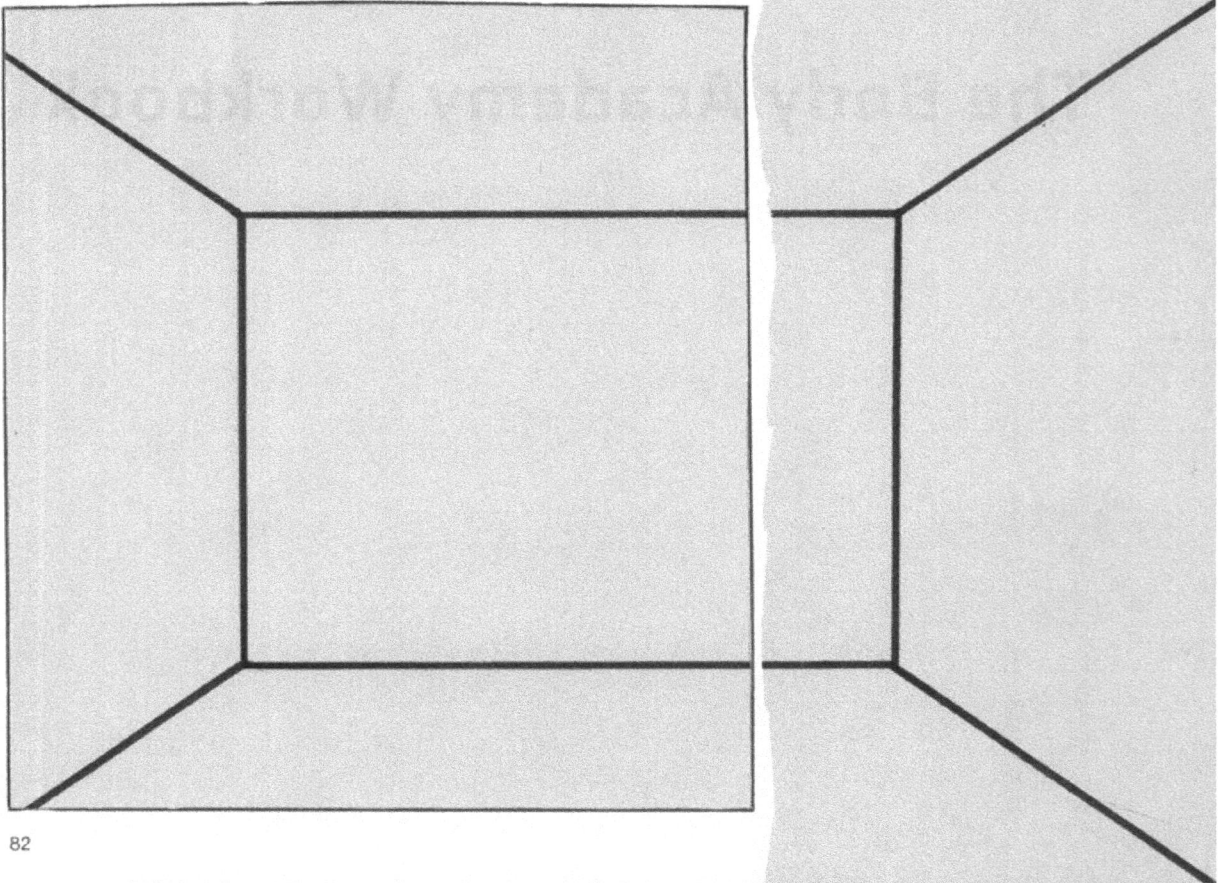

82

From July to October 2000, more than 900 women from around the world gathered in Germany to attend seminars taught by women scientists and feminist scholars such as Patricia Williams, Emily Martin, Veena Das, Sumathi Ramaswamy, M. Jacqui Alexander, Nelly Oudshoorn, and Patricia McFadden. It was officially the pilot semester of the International Women's University, organized into six academies: Body, City, Information, Migration, Water, and Work.

After the "pilot" semester was over and 900 women returned home, the project quietly and slowly ceased to exist, with hardly a trace left.

This sequence is a look back and forward. Notes taken and lines of poems written during the Body Academy lectures at the turn of the century collide with textual fragments scribbled years later in search of utopia and revolt. The future is unwritten.

Patricia W. Says

As I reflect on this belief structure in store windows, my nose slides around on my face and my eyes drip to my chin. This decision was appealed. It assumes that psyche is not a significant part of a whole. I must look.

Action

You saw a movement leader in a frame
of children refugees and refugee mothers.
TV screen the outer boundary.
Leader, camera, signal, antenna,
cables, screen, and your central
nervous system.
Noses, eyes, images of water
dripping down trees.

Emily Says

Images of the body as a machine abound. Immunologists barricaded behind the body's walls. Who is friend and who is foe, which is safe territory. You are responsible and powerless workers. Climb sheer walls and slender tall poles, cross high wires, and jump off cliffs on zip wires with the management.

Action

It's an era of ebbing aspirations.
Also once again—spring.
You plant wild greens
and edible mushrooms
between two benches
in a new, unnamed public park.

Veena Says

War is a contract. Motherhood a part of the nationalist repertoire. Mourning is a way of remembering. Of remembering pain, body, language. Family is a site of love and oppression. Victimization a breath cycle.

Action

Bharat Mata and Mother Earth design
protest placards every night and take
to the streets each percussive morning. Try
to halt traffic, cause trouble
everywhere. But no one sees them.
They wear white cotton and wool robes,
AC filters as hats, and they made it snow
under this glass dome
surrounded by the sea.
In clear water full of microscopic life,
Mothers laugh, buoyant and luxurious. Try.

Sumathi Says

Colonial rule demands map-mindedness. The globe is not space, but the sea and the sky. Another Earth. One cannot defeat an enemy without becoming at least a little alike. State orders graphics, cartoons, poems, visual salvation, clothing, a geo-body to relate to.

Action

State lets in refugees in waves.
State kicks out refugees again.
Bourgeois hydrangeas forget their
origins. Can each petal become a citizen?
Marriage again marriage and
again marriage. You are against
everything. You offer this
fruit fetish, this slice of life.

M. Jacqui Says

All of us inherit all of the earlier historical moments. No process touches one person without touching the other. Our bodies bear all markings of power.

Action

Tried to defeat enemies, became a bit
like them. (Try again.)
Your breaths bear all
markings of power. Administrative
borders drawn in postcolonial times
cut through your lungs.
Children learn to see animals
as property and kin at once.
Storms click with the mass
of sensual land. Try again.

Nelly Says

Scientists create the reality of the body. Now technologies transform bodies. Dissolve the distinction between inside and outside. Boundaries of fertility shift.

.

Action

Skin chafes against skin, to dial and
release is more sensual.
This is what you learned
during your first revolution.
Dissolve the distinction
between inside and outside.
It comes down to reflexes
as your lens attracts light,
and spectrum waves wash over the film.
Change is when and what.
You drove through a new,
unnamed tunnel your first day
of freedom from the jail to the clinic
to your studio in the downtown womb.
Folks knew what they saw when
your billboards would enter their fields.
Now everyone holds private carnivals,
adapts to new paradigms.

Patricia M. Says

I locate, re-enter, re-locate. Never with a broken back, never a shred without broken eggs. Taboos, "delicate" rituals, missiles. A heavy debt burden plays itself out in the lives of poor women.

Fake City

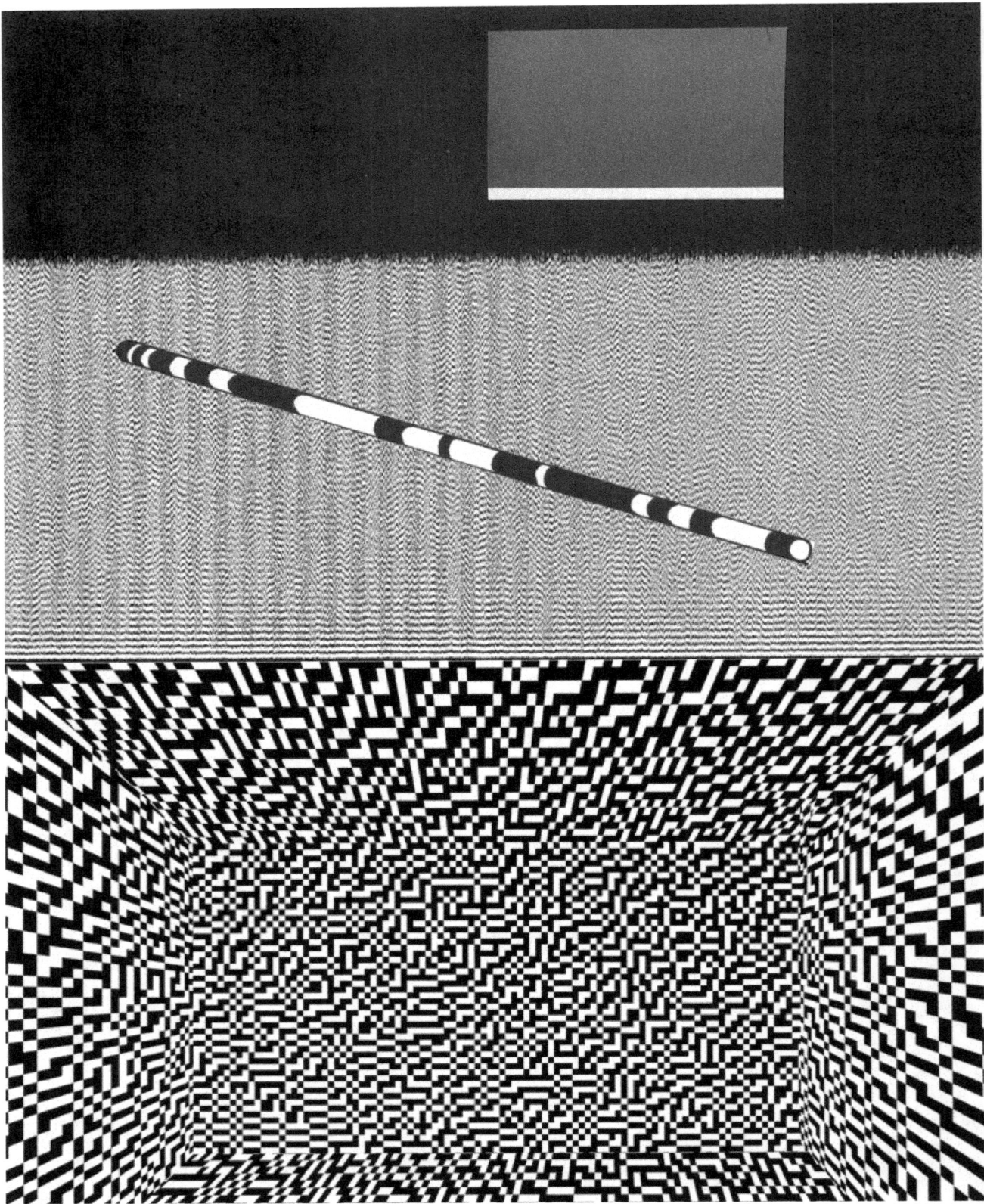

Fixed locations give way to a continuous process of locating, not only through critiques of naming and address but also through the poem itself as one of many multi-rhythmed processes that bring bodies and cities, if temporarily, into alignment and connection.

Zoë Skoulding, Bangor, Wales

What if there was no "space," only a permanent, slow-motion mystic takeover, an implausibly careening awning? Nothing is utopian. Everything wants to be.

Lisa Robertson, unlocated

South Shore

You appear blind to these crones whose art museum is this expanse of dunes. They walk along the lake in Indiana, gaze over to the Chicago skyline across and think, "Yeah, we got a glass dome for that." They curate self-portrait series in dark brown wood stumps and installations of kites in fragments of the blue midday sky. They let reflections overlap with shadows. Between steel mills and the woods, they map your parkland in orange, green, white, and grey. Videos of dystopias star kites and dying industries alike.

Between Two El Stops

I took off my red hat at Chicago
and put on my purple hat at Division

anyone who gets on now
will have no concept

of my red hat
stashed in my book bag

El

All of us on the platform were unknown kin.
Our shoes new turquoise or frayed red,
canvas stitched together, rubber glued on by our kin.
The upwardly mobile were drunk at 9 pm on a Wednesday,
full of baked, grilled or otherwise cooked flesh,
grains, tubers, and fungi.
On the east platform
a man started to speak.
His white turtleneck sweater a square of blank space
to be filled with meaning later
much later.
On the west platform
(I was there too)
Sonia Sanchez gave a talk
even though someone
or something had
turned off her mic.
She was everyone's kin
she wore print
and knits
and fire.

Ghost Town in Reverse

Only sailors from Hugo Pratt's comics visit her
lakeshore and riverbanks. Among yellow bulldozers
that never miss the subterranean urban vein,
elderly denizens of coffee shops transmit messages. Witness.

Unsafe by her corner window, she studies the rhythm
of drawbridges and the slow motion of freighters. Her skin
smells of her kitchen. I cross the tracks and drift farther
away from fried poultry. Sixteen stages of the wind
whip the asphalt between us.

The Ghost Book

*

18th Place, a patch of its asphalt stripped,
unearths steel tracks
of a ghost streetcar system
long gone before the oldest part of me
hit the scene—so why does it feel like a loss?

*

Yesterday a building burned on the Far South Side.
From passing cars, eyes could see smoke in sunset
yellowish grey and mad
and all around
the block was blinking with
fire truck lights, a troubled bee colony of them.

*

The rails under the street appear to be of pre-Sneža Žabić formation.
The word "ghost" appears to be of pre-Germanic formation.
The sense of pre-Sneža Žabić Chicago should be fury, anger
The sense of pre-Germanic ghoizdo-z should be fury, anger
I particularly like Avestan *zōi̡ da*—"ugly" and how
"outside Germanic the derivatives point to a primary sense
'to wound, tear, pull to pieces'"

*

What if I return and find my building
a burning copycat? Six years or more
of possessions of our meager life gone.
And the two of us embraced in mutual comfort.

*

The next day an outpouring of charity
from family, friends, and acquaintances,
a fresh start, and new neuroses to do with disasters.

*

After the fire
you wear someone's old clothes

*

These fingers type
what I tell them to
later they'll remember
what I no longer possess
but they won't have a language

*

The sounds the child-me would hear
came from magpies
of Eurasia, North Africa, maybe even North America
svraka, magpie, *pica pica*
imitating sirens
when days passed
without ambulances and fire trucks
magpies mocked cuckoos
kukavica, cuckoo, *cuculus*

Translation 1

Three-story walkups, Virgin Mary shrines, holidays on the street, taste or smell. It's Monday morning in my dream, tomorrow the world. They can never prove or smell in my dream, but I feel bodies touching. There are no cars, no red fire hydrants. A free city. Land bulldozed away. Pure clay and sand. Smooth. A cow gallops past.

Translation 2

My god is no saint. My dream is to wake up early in the morning around the world in my sleep. I cannot taste or smell never. But touching the body. Narrow sidewalk maintenance. Hard hats discovered the asphalt. Urban, bulldozed dirt cube, blocks away. Soft clay and sand. My friend, I met a tall iron gate. Gallop past a cow.

Translation 3

I dream of Pilsen three-story walkups, Virgin Mary shrines in front yards. There are no mothers of god, no saints. It's morning in the waking world enveloping my sleep. I can never taste or smell in my dream, but I sense bodies touching. I keep to the narrow strip of pavement to the right. There are no cars, no red fire hydrants, no small young ash trees, no sidewalk. Hard hats must have dug out the asphalt, a city block sized cube of dirt bulldozed away. Clay and smooth sand. I meet my friends in front of a broad, tall, cast-iron gate, left ajar. A cow gallops past.

Translation 4

The world surrounded me. Sleep. Holidays on the street. Their physical contact, leveled soil. Speeding past a cow.

Machine

an imagined compass
a made-up bird
black and red
true, true

Militant

Militant clouds and spray cans
are the city's tools today.

Train windows are comic
book panels. Station after station
bodies pressed close in the positive
charge of sweat. How can there be peace.
How can there be conscious flesh.

Graphite puddles convene in gutters.
How can there be movement.

Tower

here we are in a welter of fellow artifacts at the foot
of a tower grafted with crumbles of its conquered world

elliptical and unfinished, I am lifted,
a two-dimensional egg slice on a billboard

Trace Wonder

my name my idea
my target split before
and after

that loom minds
this middle broil
touches mimics
some dweller of this capital city
this battle zone

peripheral war is present
some deep rupture
some brush
in these margins
of my native haunt

this voice constructs form
from trace wonder

Lottie Claiborne in the Snake Pit

The chord changes came in like a new coat of asphalt on the avenue where I was born. These cities are paved-over marshes and prairies. Warehouse windows suffer damage each time there's a big hailstorm. As a matter of fact I consider myself the best exotic dancer in the world. They called me Lottie the Body. It was before or around the time of live recordings with two drum sets. Or two pianos accompanying one another. The chords were jazz, but the rhythm fit the blues.

System

It comes naturally in the 21st century, the world is exhausted, you're a tourist here. On the menu are pickled jalapeños. Beans and barley have been sorted, soaked, rinsed, pressure cooked. Eggs were poached in a stew of onions, peppers, garlic, and tomato. In leftover boxes, fettuccine primavera. There's soup, there are mixed greens, balsamic vinegar and olive oil.

One day years ago my hosts in LA gave me a canvas bag full of oranges grown in their front yard. I carried them on the train to Long Beach City, and the trail ends there. A version of me in LA County survives on oranges and avocados harvested from people's yards. I imagine a pair of hands and a small sharp knife. There's a rag to clean up the mess, a parachute handkerchief that unfolds like a rose.

A Cheap Fix

You come to work each day to pound metal into submission. Save for airfare and a fleabag bed. You're an untitled black and white photograph in 1969. Hold a small white feather between thumb and finger, and even your hands look like wings of a white bird. It's the light and shadows on your skin. You're learning how to become a baker, or maybe a typist, or maybe a computer programmer. A new age is about to begin and then end, and then another one, and then another one. There has never been a plan for this part of the city. There was one, but no one looked at it. Have a jelly donut and black coffee. It's a cheap fix for hunger mixed with exhaustion. Eat sitting down, Egyptian scribe style.

Industrial Land

This page is haunted by
the figure of a young
woman approaching
factory gates
somewhere in industrial land

she is a daughter of
proletarians and still
lives at home

her hair is clean
parted in the middle
curly and dyed red
by the sun
still rising

the hem of her purple wool skirt
above her knee cap

an alter ego
of a much younger you
her life is
an unlit matchstick
and her pen
could write alternate endings
to Andersen's tales

in a green bound volume
on the small shelf
by her single bed

this page skirts
the Atlantic
and the North Sea

this page is crisscrossed with
tram tracks, cables
and utility poles

The Breath Capital

Large undulating crowds move along the grid of this houndstooth city, in tubes of our metropolitan pipe organ beneath the surface, and along all the elevated tracks.

Illusion of control in the life project of minimal expectations.

You rent a flat and try to decipher mysterious messages etched in the cracks in the drywall: alphabet characters, abstracted quarter notes, and a constellation of nails, each small silver head a possibility.

The green ash tree paints over ever larger portions of the sky. Come November, its branches bare, a lattice of twigs will crisscross the theater marquee a block over. The neighborhood will cling to its past of half-lit neon signs.

Span

We complete our purchases and note the air-conditioned flow of particles through our breathing apparatuses.

Cashiers and security guards, visible labor.

Maintenance staff, light sources and shadows at once.

When the eldest one of us was born, future was a carnival and parrots rode motorcycles. A lifespan can be impossibly long.

Slight breeze, humidity, clouds like crumpled aluminum foil.

Elsewhere, a marathon runner raised awareness today by letting her blood flow stain her crotch. It's here, she said, linearity and brokenness.

The aluminum foil is smoothened and burnt.

Heal like a fractured bone, child.

Acknowledgements

"Spirit," "Limbs" (as "Friends and Monsters"), "With It," and "Paper Finger Manifesto" appear in *Cedars*, Issue 4, 2013.

"The Ghost Book" appears in *Word for Word*, Volume 21, 2011.

Snežana Žabić is the author of the short story collection *In a Lifetime* (KOS, Belgrade, Serbia, 1996), the poetry collection *Po(eat)ry* (SKC NS, Novi Sad, Serbia, 2013) written with Ivana Percl, and the hybrid memoir *Broken Records* (punctum books, USA, 2016). Her prose and poetry have appeared in *Feminist Review*, *Copper Nickel*, *Coconut*, *RealPoetik*, and elsewhere. Her poetry is included in the anthologies *Discursive Bodies of Poetry: Poetry and Poetics by a New Generation of Women Poets*, edited by Dubravka Đurić et al. (AŽIN, Belgrade, 2004) and *Cat-Painters: An Anthology of Contemporary Serbian Poetry from the Sixties to the Present*, edited by Dubravka Đurić and Biljana Obradović (Dialogos Press, New Orleans, 2016). Her writing has been translated into Macedonian, Hungarian, Polish, Swedish, and Croatian.

In the late 1990s in Belgrade, Serbia, Snežana took part in AŽIN's School of Poetry and Poetics, a project dedicated to radical poetic practice and the study of critical theory and historical avant-garde movements. In that same time period, she was a founder of LitKon, the first network for the literary exchange among newly formed post-Yugoslav states. In the early 2000s in Croatia, she co-founded Neo AFŽ, a radical feminist and anti-nationalist activist group. She attended graduate school in Hungary and Germany before obtaining her MFA at the University of North Carolina at Wilmington and her PhD at the University of Illinois at Chicago. She edits *Packingtown Review*.

www.ingramcontent.com/pod-product-compliance
Lightning Source LLC
Chambersburg PA
CBHW081157090426
42736CB00017B/3357